To: Lesslie,

I am you..
You are Me..
Together, We are the Light

Much Love,
[signature]

4-17-17

6th Sense & Purpose
The Power in Knowing Who You Are

From the great-granddaughter of a much loved House Servant... To My Mama Essie... With eternal love and gratitude for all you represented throughout your live here on earth! I take great pride in the opportunities that I have today because of your wholesome participation in the ultimate "sacrifice" and "leadership" during a time and space where the "skies were not always blue" in life! I live because you loved so dearly and profoundly!

It is with "great honor" and privilege to dedicated my first book of knowledge to You and the life you lived just for Me, so now I give a small gift back to you and the world today to know, value & protect the "inherent blessings" that we all have stored within"! I love you... *your little princess...Phrantceena*

My Great-Grandmother, "Mama Essie A. Tate", served the family of Senator Sam J Ervin, one of our US most famed and notable Senators from Morganton, NC. The two special notations below represent handwritten notes to Phrantceena on March 22, 1993 and the second most recent tribute in 2014, from the daughter of Senator Sam J Ervin, Ms. Laura Smith and Ms. Dottie Ervin, the niece of Senator Sam J. Ervin regarding her "Mama Essie".

Phrantceena

"Thank you for your tribute to Essie. She was like a second mother to me and more. Essie would have been so proud of you and what you have achieved and will accomplish in the years to come.

Cordially, Sam J. Ervin, III dated: March 22, 1993."

Further reading on this published article and a practical tribute from Senator Sam J. Ervin, can be found in "The Heritage of Burke County" – attributed to the Heritage Volume I at the Burke County Library.

Phrantceena

"Dottie shared the 1st chapter of your I AM series with me - The Power of Knowing Who You Are. I am sure your books will be wonderfully motivational for children and families in developing confidence in their own personhood and abilities. This coupled with your own wonderful life story should be a great help especially to young people starting out. (When you get to be my advanced age what I am trying to do is to lose ego and separateness and become part of the Divine Suchness.) What a beautiful portrait of you too! I know your Great-Grandmother would be so proud. I will return your copy to Historic Burke. Dottie and I agreed that any introduction regarding Essie would be Dad's tribute to her in the Burke County Heritage Volume I. All you would need to do is to attribute it to the heritage volume. I enjoyed meeting you and am most impressed with what you are doing with your writing.

Laura Smith, daughter of Senator Sam J. Ervin and Dottie Ervin, niece of Senator Sam J. Ervin" dated: October 3, 2014

Our 6th Sense & Purpose

The Power in Knowing Who You Are

Phrantceena T. Halres

Copyright © 2015 Phrantceena T. Halres.

All rights reserved. No part of this book may be used or reproduced by any means, graphic, electronic, or mechanical, including photocopying, recording, taping or by any information storage retrieval system without the written permission of the publisher except in the case of brief quotations embodied in critical articles and reviews.

Archway Publishing books may be ordered through booksellers or by contacting:

Archway Publishing
1663 Liberty Drive
Bloomington, IN 47403
www.archwaypublishing.com
1 (888) 242-5904

Because of the dynamic nature of the Internet, any web addresses or links contained in this book may have changed since publication and may no longer be valid. The views expressed in this work are solely those of the author and do not necessarily reflect the views of the publisher, and the publisher hereby disclaims any responsibility for them.

Any people depicted in stock imagery provided by Thinkstock are models, and such images are being used for illustrative purposes only.
Certain stock imagery © Thinkstock.

ISBN: 978-1-4808-1630-5 (sc)
ISBN: 978-1-4808-1632-9 (hc)
ISBN: 978-1-4808-1631-2 (e)

Library of Congress Control Number: 2015903937

Print information available on the last page.

Archway Publishing rev. date: 3/17/2015

CONTENTS

Introduction xi

PART 1: BEING EVERYWHERE BUT COMING FROM NOWHERE

Chapter 1 Eight Simple Truths We Have Already Forgotten 3
Chapter 2 Knowing Who You Are, Defined 19
Chapter 3 The Psyche of Others 26
Chapter 4 The Struggle Part I: Who Everyone Needs You to Be 36
Chapter 5 The Struggle Part II: Who Your Situation Wants You to Be 46

PART 2: GOING TO SOMEWHERE

Chapter 6 Do You Think You *Already* Know Who You Are? 54
Chapter 7 Discovering Who You Are 60
Chapter 8 Fifteen Benefits in Knowing Who You Are 67
Chapter 9 People Changers versus People Enhancers 72
Chapter 10 Being Yourself Fully versus Becoming More of Who You Are 78
Chapter 11 Taking Who You Are on the Road 83

PART 3: NOW HERE, NOW WHAT?

Chapter 12 When Who You Are Changes, Again 90
Chapter 13 When You Forget Who You Are 96
Chapter 14 Helping Others Discover Who They Are 102
Chapter 15 Trusting Yourself, Trusting Others 107
Chapter 16 Conclusion 113

The Fullness of I Am – The Message Expressed

We are all created in the reflection of God. In that reflection we are love, strength, wholeness, peace, happiness, success, and truth. Embracing the reality of who you are through the embodiment of the *I Am* series is the start of re-experiencing your greatest and fullest life—*today*. It is my wish through this series to give you back to yourself, one book at a time. It is my goal to take subjects that have been demonstrated as complex and create a simple yet divine understanding for you, the reader. Allow the *I Am* series to show you the foundation of rediscovering your fundamental nature, your real identity—your essence.

I Am: 6th Sense & Purpose

- **Love:** The Power in Knowing Who You Are

- **Strength**: The Art of Holding Your Internal Power Through External Crises

- **Wholeness**: The Joy in Living on Purpose Every Single Day

- **Peace**: The Freedom in Keeping It Simple

- **Happiness**: The Key to Living on Less While Harvesting More

- **Success**: The Beauty in Bringing the Change You Wish to See in the World

- **Truth**: The Esteem in Sharing Your Knowledge

The *I Am* series employs a concept I've coined known as the "Adult as the Teacher," whereby it offers an adult, teen, and children's version of the same book. As adults are learning, so, too, they are teaching teens and children. The goal is to ensure continuous growth as an individual and familial unit through reading each book.

Within each book title listed above, pay special attention to the Family-Owned Course Understanding Segment (FOCUS) at the end of each chapter. Its goal is to initiate the Adult as the Teacher concept in an easily usable and understandable manner. The FOCUS is intended to present family exercises, conversational topics for discussion, and actionable items in a manner to engage the entire family. Whether you have an unconventional family or a traditional one, please—each one, teach one.

In conclusion, it is my dream that this series does not end with these seven creeds. I wish the world to know who they are and to join the journey with inputs to their truths. My vision is that this *I Am* series will be never-ending.

Your journey starts here. It starts now. Welcome to the experience. Let us rediscover *love*.

Love: *The Power in Knowing Who You Are*

INTRODUCTION

> I am ... the secret to all things: the love, the power, the freedom I seek ... I discovered it within me ... and it can be frightening to know that I have just begun to rediscover the treasury chest within ... and today and every day I will continue to embrace it all from within to radiant without ... I give you back to you—a precious gift to treasure ...
>
> —Phrantceena T. Halres

Somewhere, somehow, we have allowed the light within us to flicker, sway, and often dim. We have forgotten how wonderful, beautiful, powerful—how *full*—we really are. It is not that the light is burning out; it has only been hidden. See, darkness is merely the absence of light. And behind the stereotypes, expectations, roles, rejections, and judgments that we face daily, *there*—still burning—is our own light blazing intensely and mightily. That light is who we are, and it is waiting to shine brightly once again and to expand into all other areas, bringing clarity, vision, and purpose—not only to our personal lives, but in the lives of those around us.

I am no great philosopher. I am no famously recognized spiritual guru, nor do I try to be. I'm purely a witness and a testament to the power of the source within myself. This book (*and the series*) allows me to share my truth. I wish for the one now reading this book to know that the same source that resides within me is the same source that resides within you. You don't need to seek it.

Your only goal is to become aware of it and to allow its expression everywhere you go. Don't worry if you don't know how. I'll show you.

Throughout this book, I share with you my own stories in hopes that you find a relationship with me through similarities we share. I've lived for years confused about my own identity. My truth about who I really was, was hidden deep within me. Because of this, I went through cycles of struggle, frustration, confusion, and pain. My wish for you is to end your cycle of struggle sooner than I did and to live a life full of joy, with relationships experienced fully and abundance you never could have imagined … all because you know who you are.

Love: The Power in Knowing Who You Are is a foundational message. It is a communication on remembering instead of on learning. It is about clearing space instead of creating additions. It is about disconnecting with fear and reconnecting to love. It is about becoming less of *them* and more of you. It is about reigniting the power, strength, courage, and confidence in that journey.

Are you ready to begin?

Part One
Being Everywhere but Coming from Nowhere

Chapter One
Eight Simple Truths We Have Already Forgotten

What people believe prevails over the truth.

—Sophocles

I knew at a very young age that something was different within me. Although this *something* is a blessing now, at the time I felt it to be a curse. It was confusing. It was frustrating. It was a different type of experience than what I imagined others at my age were going through. I used to ask myself, "Why do others want me to feel afraid when I do not?"

"Why do others want me to feel less valuable than I feel at this very moment?"

We are all uniquely created. But it is through our uniqueness that we are alike and that we are connected. We connect through aspirations, talents, wants, and desires, but did you also know that we connect at levels very deep within? We connect in ways that are central to our core. We were born with gifts that go unbeknownst to us, untapped, unused. I will explain this later, but for now, here are eight simple truths that many of us have *long* forgotten:

We are strong: Have you ever seen documentaries about natural disasters that have occurred all around the world? *What about those who endured them*—those who were left with only the clothes on their back … no home, no food, no money, and some even experiencing the loss of loved ones. Not only did they survive the devastation of the natural disaster, but they survived the devastation of needing to create a new life.

We are strong. We were all born with the will to survive, to endure, and to overcome.

You *are strong!*

We are powerful: Have you ever observed a motivational speaker as he or she entered the zone? Have you watched as a speaker took center stage and engaged an audience? Have you ever noticed the stillness of the crowd as they followed the speaker's every word and as they clung to each portion of wisdom the speaker offered? What an amazing power this speaker has. The energy, the connection … *the power* that some motivational speakers have to move audiences is astonishing.

We are powerful. We were all born powerful. We have the power to move mountains, to part rivers, and ultimately to create the desires of our heart.

You *are powerful!*

We are creative: Have you ever watched an artist? Have you ever seen anyone begin with nothing but a blank piece of paper and end with a masterpiece? People do it every single day. Painters, architects, writers, entrepreneurs, and strategists all create something out of what was once nothing.

We are creative. We were all born with the authority to breathe life into ideas, thoughts, feelings, people, places, and things.

You *are creative!*

We are attractive: Have you ever wondered how when we are doing good, we are doing really good, but it seems like when we are doing bad … boy, are we doing really bad? Did you know that we are like magnets? As a matter of fact, we are just like magnets. We have charges that run through us called energy that creates a magnetic field around us. This magnetic field attracts. Our energy attracts, and it detracts. It brings things our way, and it pushes things away from us. This happens around us all the time, whether we know it or not.

We are attractive. We were born with a gift to pull toward ourselves anything and everything that we desire, and to push away those things that are undesirable.

You *are attractive!*

We are deserving: Have you ever watched how homeless people are sometimes treated? Because they have no home and no money, there are many who feel that they deserve no food either. Must one result in the other? Should a person have a job, a home, and a steady income in order to be worthy of at least food and water? There are some who believe that simply because they lack certain elements in their life—a degree, certain physical features, a high credit rating—that they are undeserving and unworthy of other things like certain jobs, lifestyles, people, or feelings. Should one always produce another? No.

Simply because we were born, we are deserving of all that is great in our world. We are even deserving of *defining* what is great in our world. We were born with the right to be, do, and have all that is good.

You *are deserving!*

We are beautiful: Have you ever visited a botanical garden? It can almost take your breath away, right? The beauty of these gardens is no different than the beauty of wonders of the world, like a waterfall, a canyon, a cave, the view from a mountaintop, a sunset, or an ocean. We can probably all agree that God's creations are beautiful. They have an intrinsic peace and an inborn beauty about them just because they exist. There is not one thing that they have to do in order to be beautiful. They just are. Merely being here and showing up for life each day grants them that authority. The same holds true for you. You, too, have an intrinsic peace and an inborn beauty that you are granted just for showing up for life. There are no other requirements, nothing more and nothing less.

We are beautiful. We were born with a natural inner beauty that has the ability to shine so brightly that it has the power to overshadow any external features or characteristics.

You *are beautiful!*

We are whole: Have you ever noticed that people who break up sometimes say, "He stole a piece of my heart when he left me," or "She stole a piece of my heart when she left me"? Although it may feel this way, in reality you were born whole, and when someone walks out of your life, you are still whole. It is not about finding anything to fill the void; it is about recognizing what is already there.

We are full, we are filled, we are complete, we are satisfied, we are total—*we are whole*. No one can complete us or take away from us.

We were born complete. Any addition to us is not a completion; it is a bonus. There are those who can make us feel like more of ourselves or add to our already complete spirit, but there is no one on earth who can complete us—because we are already whole.

You *are whole!*

We are loved: Have you ever witnessed a parent's love for a child? Time and time again, I've heard the saying, "You never know love until you have had a child." A parent's love for his or her child can be unconditional, unwavering, and evermore forgiving. It is the type of love that transcends thought or meaning. A parent's love cannot be learned in textbooks or taught in classrooms. It is purest when it is natural.

We were born in the image of love and to be loved. We were born deserving and worthy of love.

You *are loved!*

Do you understand how this works now? Are you wondering, "Where was I when this course was taught?"

The truth of the matter is that most people have forgotten just how powerful, creative, attractive, deserving, beautiful, whole, and loved they are. With a foundation so warped and confused, this image and identity problem starts to spread into all other areas of life. Are there any areas in your life where you experience fear, intimidation, jealousy, or unworthiness? These are not experienced because you are a failure of some kind. These are experienced because you are having a crisis of identity. If you were able not only to remember but also to accept these basic, simple truths, you would already be on your way to creating a fuller, richer, and more vibrant life.

Now, if you are wondering if all of these things that I tell you are true, all you really need to do in order to seek confirmation is to watch our generation of babies and *most* toddlers. As a matter of fact, if you have children this age, try observing them today. Our babies will dance when no one is looking—*and when everyone is looking*. They will sing (in baby noises, of course) their little hearts away if they love a song. They will not look around to see who is watching. They will laugh at themselves in the mirror and chew on their toes if it makes them happy. Our children are full of life, and they experience it in each passing moment. Our children are so full of joy. They are full of a joy that is not dependent upon *your* joy. If they depended on your joy, how often would they truly be happy? Babies are full of a love that is not learned from the love that you have for yourself. If they learned how to love themselves by watching you, how often would they truly feel self-love? Babies are full of a peace and acceptance that that is not dependent upon your peace and acceptance for life. If they learned peace and acceptance by watching you, *would they feel it*?

If you are a parent reading this section, I do not say these things to be critical. It is to merely demonstrate the gifts that we—*all of us*—are born with. Here's the good news: we still have them today, and we do not have to do anything complex in order to have those feelings again. We just have to uncover them, dust them off, and fine-tune them a bit.

Now do you see how this works?

You are becoming aware of the power within yourself. And that is good news! See, the first step in realizing your full potential is to do an inventory of what you already have available to you. Now that you know what is already inside of who you are, let us take some time to first, uncover, second, remove, and finally extinguish all of those things that we are *not*.

End of Chapter One

FOCUS.
FAMILY-OWNED CHAPTER UNDERSTANDING SEGMENT

Current Experience
Teen: Pages [ ]: By now, your teen is learning about
Child: Pages [ ]: By now, your child has been introduced to

Conversational Topics
How do children, teens, and adults all experience these feelings differently?

What prevents us from feeling aware of these things each moment of the day?

Exercises
As a family, ask your partner and children how many of these feelings — strong, powerful, creative, attractive, deserving, whole, loved — they have felt.

Which ones have they felt more strongly than others, and which are the weakest feelings for them? When do they feel these feelings most?

Discuss as a family how to grow in the awareness of each of these feelings as you progress through the day.

Actionable Items
As a family, come up with one simple affirmation that includes each of these things we are born with. Take a moment of appreciation each day during your reading of the affirmation.

My Journal

Chapter Two
Ten Falsehoods That We Have Adopted

I was the firstborn among my siblings. There were five of us in total, but because I came first, I was caught in many situations that my siblings did not have to experience. It was no secret that my mother's side of the family was poor and my father's side was very wealthy. This gave me an opportunity to live on both sides of the track, so to speak. When I would go to see my mother's family, I would learn things like survival, common sense, and how to protect myself. On my father's side, I'd learn etiquette, the importance of education, and how to be sophisticated. Although I was such a blessed child to have experienced both sides, this dual living became central to my confusion in learning who I really was. If one side of my family was telling me that I was one thing and the other side was molding me to be another, then ... who was I? Who was I supposed to be? At that time, I didn't know.

Do you?

If we have forgotten how very strong, powerful, creative, attractive, deserving, whole, and loved we really are, then how do we currently know ourselves? How do others know themselves? As a matter of fact, if you ever sit in public and people-watch, this is a great question to ask. What image of ourselves are we presently adopting? We are adopting falsehoods. And falsehoods are nothing more than lies about who we really are. Every single day we are adopting and investing in falsehoods. And you would not believe how many falsehoods about ourselves we have adopted.

We have accepted the ideas that we are

>fearful
>
>jealous
>
>failures
>
>mediocre
>
>unworthy
>
>disabled
>
>worried
>
>unloved
>
>evil
>
>unknowing

To adopt a child is to legally obtain another's child and bring it up as one's own. To adopt a falsehood is to obtain another's negative feeling about himself or herself and bring it up as our own. As we nurture this falsehood, it (*like our adoptive children*) becomes stronger, more complex, and more front and center in our lives. This falsehood, like our nurtured children, comes first in all that we do. We then learn to see this falsehood in ourselves and in others.

Where do these images come from? From whom are we adopting these falsehoods about ourselves?

>our mothers

our fathers

our sisters

our brothers

our cousins

our aunts

our uncles

our friends

our neighbors

our coworkers

our managers

our teachers

our leaders

our television programming

And the list goes on and on.

Although we may adopt falsehoods from strangers, we typically adopt falsehoods from those we are surrounded by the most. A lot of what we currently believe about ourselves has been developed in us over time. And most people do not mean to do it. Most people do not wake up in the morning thinking about what negative experience can they plant in someone. They are not doing it intentionally. As a matter of fact, oftentimes falsehoods become so dominant in *their* lives, that they do not recognize that they are teaching it to us. It is all that they really know.

But how did they come to adopt these falsehoods? Who taught them?

       their mothers

       their fathers

       their sisters

       their brothers

       their cousins

       their aunts

       their uncles

       their friends

       their neighbors

       their coworkers

       their managers

       their teachers

       their leaders

    their television programming, etc. …

And the cycle continues.

Just like you, they are growing up in environments where falsehoods are being nurtured day in and day out. When are we being taught these falsehoods? All day long. Let's say that you are a single woman in her thirties and you just received news that you've gotten a new job offer that will be a promotional opportunity for you. It will pay $100,000 per year, and you will need to relocate almost four hours away in order to accept it. In your excitement, you take this incredible news and share it with your loved ones. You start with your parents. They may congratulate you but also express their concern for your safety living in a new state by yourself. In this, you infer that you are fragile and unable to take care of your safety. *So you take in their fear.*

Then you move on to your friends. You tell them about your new promotional opportunity. They are so excited for you and congratulate you immediately. They then proceed to tell you all about the friend that they know who moved (just as you are about to) and five months later was fired for not being able to produce. So they remind you to just be careful and cautious. In this, you infer that you are mediocre and unable to rise above terminations. *So you take in their negativity.*

You decide to announce the information to your coworkers. They congratulate you and then ask if you are certain you can handle the responsibility the new job opportunity requires. In this, you begin to wonder if you are really ready to do all this job requires. *So you take in their worry.*

And then you run into a jealous cousin who reminds you that you will get taxed so much that you won't really have any money anyway. *You take in their poverty consciousness.*

People cannot help but tell us who we are. They do not do it, because they hate us. As a matter of fact, they love us. They love us so much that they want us to be protected from all the "bad" things that are just around the corner. But the advice they give is wrapped with a cloak of fear that neither you nor the advice giver can see, until it is too late. And if you are not careful, you begin to adopt those inferences and internalize the fear just the way your loved ones have. You then decline the job offer. But imagine how it would feel to be so confident in who you are that falsehoods like these could not be planted.

Ask yourself these questions. Why is it easier to accept who we are *not*, than to know and accept who we really are? Have we taken too many classes on being humble? Have we humbled our way out of our intrinsic nature? Have we learned too many times that it is better to be quiet about our strengths and to speak loudly about our disabilities so that we can connect with others?

This state of being does nothing for you or anyone connected to you. There is so much for you to be, do, and have in this one lifetime, and the start of your journey is knowing exactly who you are. So now the only natural question left is …

What does it mean to know who I am?

Keep reading. I will teach you in the next chapter.

End of Chapter Two

FOCUS
Family-Owned Chapter Understanding Segment

Current Experience

Teen: Pages [ ]: By now, your teen is learning about

Child: Pages [ ]: By now, your child has been introduced to

Conversational Topics

How do children, teens, and adults all experience these feelings differently?

What prevents us from feeling aware of these things each moment of the day?

Exercises

As a family, ask your partner and children how many of these feelings—strong, powerful, creative, attractive, deserving, whole, loved—they have felt.

Which ones have they felt more strongly than others, and which are the weakest feelings for them? When do they feel these feelings most?

Discuss as a family how to grow in the awareness of each of these feelings as you progress through the day.

Actionable Items

As a family, come up with one simple affirmation that includes each of these things we are born with. Take a moment of appreciation each day during your reading of the affirmation.

My Journal

Chapter Three
Knowing Who You Are, Defined

> Today I choose to be a woman who is giving, loving, and at peace. I thank God that I am me, and wherever I am today, I will express this devotion to giving, loving, and feeling at peace within regardless of any outside opinion, influence, or judgment.
>
> —Phrantceena Halres

This, by far, is my favorite chapter because it allows me to articulate my message for the entire book. Because this is at the top of my personal creed list, I'm often asked, "What does it mean to know who you are, Phrantceena?" For so long, I've been telling people that it is very difficult to articulate what it means to know who you are. To some things, there is no logic, rhyme, or reason. There is no meaning. There is no best way to understand it other than to feel it, and for a long time, I thought the same thing of this.

In my mind, to know who you are means to live who you are. And how many would fully understand this without (rightfully) asking more questions. So, as I sat and pondered how to articulate what it means to know who you are, the thought finally came to me.

Knowing who you are means accepting who you are choosing to be today, receiving it with appreciation, and taking your choice authentically and boldly everywhere you go.

Although this appears to be a complex notion, once it is dissected, you will see that it is very simple yet extremely powerful. Let's dissect.

Accepting who you are choosing to be today
When you wake up each morning, who or what do you choose to be? Were you even aware that you had a choice? When I say this, I am not referring to concepts such as father, mother, son, daughter, teacher, cashier, or athlete. These are the roles that we play day in and day out. I am, instead, referring to the adjective that you place in front of those roles. You have a choice on the answer to the question of, "What kind?" What kind of father do you choose to be today? What kind of mother do you choose to be today? Do you choose to be a happy daughter, a kind son, an excited teacher, or a funny cashier? Do you choose to be a giving mother, or a thoughtful father? Maybe you woke up this morning and decided that you want to be free of all roles today. Don't just be free, be happily free of all roles. *Be fancy-free* the way you would if you were on vacation for an entire day!

Focus on today. Do not worry about yesterday, and do not even think about tomorrow. Yesterday is what it was, and tomorrow will be what it will be. Today is yours for the making. Have optimism in today. Find power in the moment. Discover love in your present.

And whatever you choose to be today, accept it fully. Embrace it with love and excitement. Accept it with the same bright eyes and anticipation that you used to feel as a child on the eve of holidays like Christmas. Accept it with full knowing that it will be, simply because you have a desire for it to manifest in this manner.

Receiving it with appreciation

Once you've chosen who you wish to be today and you have fully embraced it with love and excitement, learn to receive it with appreciation.

To receive something means to allow, entertain, or accept it. Think, for example, of people who are given compliments. Some people receive compliments day in and day out, but they still have the lowest self-esteem. Why? It is mostly because although they are given compliments, they do not receive them. They do not allow, entertain, or accept the notion that their dress is beautiful, or their smile is remarkable, or their work was meticulous. Every compliment that is given is knocked down by a barrier.

We do the same with the choices we make for who we wish to be. We may go the added mile and affirm the choice to be a thoughtful father, but just as quickly as the choice was made, we think of five reasons why today is not the best day to start this process: we have to stay over at work, the kids got on our nerves yesterday and they need to be taught a lesson, or some other reason. It is in this moment that we resist our own choices. But I am challenging you to make a change. Do the opposite today. Instead of looking for reasons to delay the process, look for reasons to entertain the process. Think of the benefits of staying on the path to being a thoughtful father.

And once you receive it, learn to appreciate it. Always know that everything you appreciate grows. The more you learn to appreciate your lifestyle choices, the happier, prouder, and more confident you will become. The more confident you become, the more others learn to respect, value, and appreciate your aura of fullness. And the more others learn to respect, value, and appreciate your aura of fullness, the less likely they are to challenge your decision to choose who you wish to be. As a matter of fact, they, too, learn the gift of choosing for themselves. And the cycle continues … yet this time, in a positive way.

Taking your choice authentically and boldly with you wherever you are

Take your choices everywhere you go. If your choice is to be a happy woman, be that. Be as happy as your heart desires. Do not concern yourself with what is happening around you. The strongest type of happiness comes not because of what is happening around you. It is in spite of what is happening around you. Learn to be happy wherever you go instead of waiting for outside influences to make you happy. Outside influences creating happiness may be few and far between, but if you choose to be happy everywhere you go, you will start seeking happiness in everything. You will start looking for reasons to smile, creating reasons to laugh, and attracting to yourself reasons to jump up and down with excitement. Take your happiness everywhere you go.

Be bold and authentic with what you have chosen to feel. Be unapologetic. Be unashamed. Many people believe that they must stoop or bend in order to uplift others. For instance, they may believe that they must hide their level of happiness in order to help someone who is sad. But just the opposite is true. I am a believer that you can inspire others to reach your level, whether it be happiness, peace, joy, love, or other positive feelings. You do not need to find drama in order to help someone discover peace. You do not need to return to hate in order to help someone find love. Be the good that you wish to see in the world and inspire others to follow your path by simply, boldly, and authentically being who you are.

Knowing who you are means accepting who you are choosing to be today, receiving it with appreciation, and courageously and authentically taking your choice everywhere you go.

Knowing who you are is one of the most powerful tools you can have on your side. When you know who you are, no one can ever tell you that you are something else. Well, they can try, but it will not work. Knowing who you are will never stop people from calling you names like stupid, cowardly, ugly, crazy, or even worse, names that are derogatory like whore, slut, and heifer. But knowing who you are, instead, prevents you from internalizing these opinions, judgments, and influences. It will prevent you from adopting those falsehoods as your own sense of self. Knowing who you are means that you do not need anyone else's definition of you, because you have your own.

So now that you know what it means to know who you are, we are going to talk a little in the next chapter about how others perceive us and why they feel a need to help us define ourselves.

End of Chapter Three

FOCUS
Family-Owned Chapter Understanding Segment

Current Experience
Teen: Pages [ ]: By now, your teen is learning about

Child: Pages [ ]: By now, your child has been introduced to

Conversational Topics
How do children, teens, and adults experience these feelings differently?

What prevents us from feeling aware of these things each moment of the day?

Exercises
As a family, ask your partner and children how many of these feelings—strong, powerful, creative, attractive, deserving, whole, loved—they have felt.

Which ones have they felt more strongly than others, and which are the weakest feelings for them? When do they feel these feelings most?

Discuss as a family how to grow in the awareness of each of these feelings as you progress through the day.

Actionable Items
As a family, come up with one simple affirmation that includes each of these things we are born with. Take a moment of appreciation each day during your reading of the affirmation.

My Journal

Chapter Four
The Psyche of Others

An ordinary people being extraordinary
—Phrantceena T. Halres

Now that you understand the importance of knowing who you are, you have an important opportunity to better understand the challenges you face with others who have a strong belief that they know who you are.

Question: Why would someone even care who you are choosing to be today?

Answer: Because it could confuse their original thought of whom they believed you to be.

To begin, let's turn our attention to textbook definitions of the following words: *discriminate*, *prejudge*, and *stereotype*. To discriminate means to perceive or constitute the difference in or between. To prejudge means to form a judgment on (an issue or person) prematurely and without adequate information. To stereotype means to make a widely held, but fixed and oversimplified, image or idea of a particular type of person or thing.

Why do other people discriminate, prejudge, and stereotype?

To answer that question, I'll have to let you in on a secret. You, too, discriminate, prejudge, and stereotype. Now, you may not do it in a way that is overtly detrimental to others, but to a certain extent, everyone prejudges, discriminates, and stereotypes. How else would we make decisions beforehand about things like dangerous situations versus safe situations? It is almost like looking through one of those high-tech goggles that have radar that scopes out an environment and the people within. It scans the room for possible signs of threat. And based on patterns, which have a connection to stereotypes, they are able to discriminate between safe and dangerous situations and can prejudge whether or not a situation would be okay to enter. If it is dangerous, the radar flashes red, indicating danger. If it is safe, the radar flashes green, indicating safety.

If you were able to understand that example, you can understand how discriminating, prejudging, and stereotyping have become survival techniques that we use. We use them all the time, and most times we do so to protect ourselves. We use them because we believe that they help us to better understand people. But this is only one side of the picture. What about the other side?

Good or bad, all of this places us in categories and in boxes that lead to others better understanding who they think we are. We already know what happens when we stop fitting categories. Others become confused, frustrated, and sometimes angry. They want to know our motive. We place people in boxes all the time. Once someone is in a box, we can say confidently that this is how they will behave, this is how they will react, this is what they will do if I do this, and this is what they will say if I say this. We've done this for so long that many times we do it without ever realizing it.

And knowing who you are presents a challenge here. In general, it could place you in a category of a limited group of people. But if you march to a different tune than most, you will stand out. Do you remember what it means to know who you are? *Knowing who you are means accepting who you are choosing to be today, receiving it with appreciation, and courageously and authentically taking your choice everywhere you go.*

Knowing who you are means breaking free of categories and labels. And the key dilemma to knowing who you are is that you are choosing who you wish to be each day, each hour, with each passing moment. And oftentimes, when society does not understand someone, they label him or her as crazy, or evil, and they hide their families so that they are not exposed to whatever tune you are marching to. Here are four clear examples of the frustration others may experience when you know who you are.

Who you wish to be may change: You have the right to change who you wish to be with every passing moment. One moment a person may wish to be a man who works in a highly conservative environment in corporate America. He goes into work each day with his three-piece suit and his cleanly shaven facial hair and haircut. The next month, he may decide that he wishes to be an artist, and instead of hiding his love for piercings, tattoos, and meaning-filled T-shirts, he'd rather expose them to the world. Although we have the right to do this, oftentimes the world is unprepared for this change in behavior, and people become frustrated because now they have to stop and place you in another category. They may begin to wonder if you have wandered off to the crazy category. Why do you believe there is such a thing as a midlife crisis? The only crisis is that they've waited until midlife to really experience their best life.

Who you wish to be may be contradictory: How can you be this and also be that? How can you be one thing and another? People believe that you should be able to be only one or the other. For example, how can this woman be both poor and joyful? How can she wear short skirts and be conservative in her thinking? How can she be nonreligious and have a close relationship with God?

Such contradictions really confuse others, and not only must they move you to a new category, they may have to create one for you. And no one wants to have to go through all that effort. They may also begin to wonder if you have wandered off to the crazy category too.

Who you wish to be may be outside of the box: *You are just different!* You march to the beat of your own drum, and you are proud of it. "Who would want to be proud being so different?" they whisper behind your back. Think of Lady Gaga. As an entertainer, she spends her time looking for new and creative ways to re-create herself differently from what most of society is used to. Her style has been known to be unorthodox, and because of that, what happens? People who are trying to place her in a category will place her in the "crazy" category.

Who you wish to be may "rub off" on others: You are evil, and this behavior is blasphemy! If you've ever heard this before, then you probably already know and understand that people are frightened by you; no one wants you to rub off on them and their loved ones. They do not want who you are choosing to be to change them. People keep their children from being exposed to things that happen all around them (e.g., addiction, sexuality) for fear of exposing them to something that they feel is not normal—although it is normal.

By now, you know that others categorize us just as much as we do or have done it to them. Others need us to fit into a paradigm. They need for us to walk a certain way, talk a certain way, dress a certain way—*act a certain way.* They need this so that they can understand us. They need this so that they are better able to figure us out. They need us to do these things so that they can know whether we are safe or dangerous.

But what if who you are choosing to be does not fit? What if you do not fit inside of one of these categories others have chosen for you? What do people do—especially to those they have placed in the "crazy" category? They try to make them "un-crazy." Our country spends billions of dollars in trying to make people appear normal again. People often try to make you fit through therapy, training, behavioral classes, interventions, and other methods. How do they do this? The five most common ways are through conditioning, manipulation, guilt, ostracism, and force.

Conditioning: During your entire life, you have been conditioned. You have been conditioned in how to speak, walk, dress, behave— *on how to conduct yourself.* There is no judgment in my statement of this. It just is. You have been trained by your family, in school, in church, at work, and even within community organizations. The conditioning may not have been overt or obvious like the way we train people in seminars and classrooms. It could have been in the form of negative or positive conditioning.

> *Positive conditioning*: Think of credentials. The more credentials you have, the more credible you are perceived to be and the more noteworthy you become. So, with that, people go on the great credential chase. They go to get their bachelor's, and then their master's, and then certifications, and then master certifications. They become prepared.
>
> *Negative conditioning*: Think of the penal system. Jails are associated with negative reinforcement. You learn to behave a certain way so that you do not find yourself behind bars.

Manipulation: Some will try to manipulate you into fitting a mold. Manipulation is no more than trying to influence you to do something that you may not have done on your own otherwise. Think of advertisements. Now, a ton of psychology goes into the creation of commercials, for instance. Marketing companies work to figure out what makes you take action so that they can cause you to take action regarding (i.e., purchase) the product or service they are selling. They will use jingles, children (especially babies), smooth-talking voices, and puppies in order to convince you to do what they wish for you to do. And it works. If it didn't, companies would not pour millions of dollars into creating them.

Guilt: Some people will try to make you feel guilty for being who you are. If you are searching for a great example, think of those living a homosexual lifestyle. Because this choice has not yet become socially acceptable in certain communities across the world, people who are homosexual are often made to feel guilty for their decision to openly express their differences.

Ostracism: Many people are ostracized into fitting a mold. Think of the young boy in school who may be different and gets picked on by all of the other children. They dislike him for his difference, whatever it may be, and they exclude him from all fun games and activities. They tease and torment him to the point where the boy begins to *believe* that something is, in fact, wrong with him and that he must change so that he can *fit in*.

Force: When you go against the grain, isn't it almost like going against gravity? And, goodness—can't gravity bring you back quickly. If you cannot be a part of a group until you behave a certain way, this becomes a form of force, especially when you feel like there aren't too many other options other than to be a part of the group. Think, for example, of living in a community. A person may not have the ability to move, and in order to live in that community, he or she must become molded to being a certain way.

Knowing who you are can prove to be a challenge to others who "thought" that they could place us into an easily understandable box.

But what are your defenses against these efforts? Is there anything you can do to safeguard yourself? Knowing who you are is a safeguard in and of itself. Knowing who you are means feeling comfortable taking you everywhere you go. When you feel that someone is trying to place you in a box that is uncomfortable to you, there are several healthy ways to cope with it.

Pay attention: Many people are simply not paying attention to what is happening around them. They are moving so quickly, minds going, and they are too busy not thinking through situations that they may have their power stolen without ever realizing it.

Remember: Always remember who you are, and take it everywhere you go. Know confidently, authentically, and boldly that who you have chosen to be is perfection. You do not need to be like everyone else in order to be accepted—to fit in.

Understand: Be aware of what is really happening around you. Understand that others try to change you as a form of protection. They try to force you into a mold because they feel that this is the only way they will be able to understand you. Either way, understanding the motive will allow you to not internalize it as much.

Ignore: For someone to say that you are something that you are not is almost as laughable as someone calling you a furry bunny when you know that you do not have bunny ears, a bunny nose, or even bunny fur. There is no way that you can be a furry bunny, because you know who you are. Just as you would ignore the comment that you are a furry bunny, so should you ignore any other comment that does not reflect who you are.

Educate: Here you have an opportunity to educate others on why you no longer fit into their box and instead fit into one that you have created for yourself. You can educate them on how your box isn't meant to be harmful to them. As a matter of fact, your box has nothing to do with them, yet everything to do with your living a full, happy, and peaceful life.

Always know that others try to fit you into a mold as a survival and a defense mechanism. This is the same reason you have done the exact same thing before. It does not make anyone right or wrong; it only means that we are all human. Do not give too much of your energy away worrying about what others think of you, especially when you have so many other things to focus your time and attention to—*such as who you choose to be tomorrow!*

So, now we have talked about the boxes that people place us in so that they can better understand who we are. Let us spend some time in the next chapter discussing who people really need us to be and why.

End of Chapter Four

FOCUS
Family-Owned Chapter Understanding Segment

Current Experience

Teen: Pages [ ]: By now, your teen is learning about

Child: Pages [ ]: By now, your child has been introduced to

Conversational Topics

How do children, teens, and adults experience these feelings differently?

What prevents us from feeling aware of these things each moment of the day?

Exercises

As a family, ask your partner and children how many of these feelings—strong, powerful, creative, attractive, deserving, whole, loved—they have felt.

Which ones have they felt more strongly than others, and which are the weakest feelings for them? When do they feel these feelings most?

Discuss as a family how to grow in the awareness of each of these feelings as you progress through the day.

Actionable Items

As a family, come up with one simple affirmation that includes each of these things we are born with. Take a moment of appreciation each day during your reading of the affirmation.

My Journal

Chapter Five
The Struggle Part I: Who Everyone Needs You to Be

Do not get lost in the crowd.

—Phrantceena T. Halres

As this book is being written, I am preparing for a speech that I am to give in coming months to a group of local women business owners. As I work to craft the most impactful speech, I often ask the question, "What do they need from me?" When they purchase their tickets and wait to hear a speech from a keynote speaker, what are they expecting to hear? What do they want to hear? What do they need to hear?

I often struggle with talking openly about my entrepreneurial ventures, awards, and accolades. Part of who I am is that I choose not to promote myself or my companies. I am not Phrantceena, business owner. I am a woman who is full of love, knowledge, joy, peace, happiness, and freedom—who happens to own a business. But marketing and public relations professionals need me to be one thing or another. Imagine it. The entire concept of PR centers on making you easily definable—memorable. And for those who wish to brand me, a very big box will be needed to fit me into. And just like PR professionals, there are others in our lives that need for us to be something. As a matter of fact, take some time and try a quick exercise for me.

> Who do you believe your mother
> wants/wanted you to be?
>
> Who do you believe your father
> wants/wanted you to be?
>
> Who do you believe your manager
> wants/wanted you to be?
>
> Who do you believe your partner
> wants/wanted you to be?
>
> Who do you believe your child(ren)
> wants/wanted you to be?
>
> Who do you believe your teacher
> wants/wanted you to be?
>
> Who do you believe your pastor/spiritual leader
> wants/wanted you to be?
>
> Who do you believe your friend(s)
> wants/wanted you to be?
>
> Who do you believe your neighbor(s)
> wants/wanted you to be?

Try to take your time in answering these questions, because they are not easy and you have probably never had to consider them previously. Consider writing the first thing that comes to mind, and try not to overthink the exercise. Once it is completed, review what you've written.

What are some thoughts that come to mind for you? Do you see any similarities in what each of them wanted you to be? Do you see any stark differences? Why do you think they had a desire for you to become any of these things? Have you actually succeeded in becoming any of them? Did you strive for any of those things and (at the time) weren't certain what your motivation was for doing so? Perhaps now you have some idea of the answers to these questions.

As a matter of fact, I answered these questions too, and I was in awe of how many people had a different idea of who I needed to be. To be fair to you, I discuss my answers below.

This was a very eye-opening exercise even for me! But always remember that the only time we get trapped into who everyone else wants us to be … is when we forget who we are.

Now, we have already talked about categories and those who need us to fit in them in order to better understand who we are and what we are up to. Oftentimes, those are the ones who don't really know us so well. The ones I'm referring to now are the ones who typically know us best. Who do they need us to be? And why do they care who we are or who we become anyway? Here's an easy answer.

Most people want us to live up to our highest potential.

Most of our loved ones want us to reach our highest potential. Now, whether one's highest potential is perceived to be great or whether it is perceived to be mediocre depends on the person you are talking to. But one thing remains the same, regardless of whom you are speaking to—they tend to believe that they know our highest potential. They want us to realize our highest potential. But therein is the issue. Consider two very common ones.

Highest potential glass ceiling: Sometimes another's perception of our highest potential isn't as high as we can really go. Some may only know success to be at a certain level. For example, if our parents have never before met someone who is rich or famous, they may never believe that people, let alone their child, have the potential to be rich and famous, regardless of how well they can sing, dance, or act.

Highest potential skew: Sometimes others want us to be who they were never able to be. And the further they strayed away from their own potential, the more important it became for us to reach our own. This could be the mother who never had an opportunity to go to college and now has a desire for her son to go to college. It could be the father who never became a football star who now pushes his son to be the next best and greatest football star. Simply because this may have been what they [insert name here] thought they were meant to be, now you are being forced to become it. And you and they are none the wiser as to what is happening. The cycle continues to repeat itself. Why do they need for us to be someone, something—our highest potential? They need this because others has/had a need for them to be someone. And the cycle continues.

And at the end of the day, like it or not, we are trading off. We are trading the power in who we are—*who we choose to be*—for something else that we desire in the moment. We are giving up our internal power in order to receive something else in return. How often are you setting aside what you are in order to give to everyone else who they want you to be. You may not believe that you are doing it, but here are some great examples. How often do you dress a certain way for work because your manager needs you to be someone? How often do you frequent certain establishments because your friends need you to be someone? How often do you strive for certain things in life because your parents need for you to be someone? And the cycle continues.

Why do we do it? Why on earth would we even care about, let alone take action on, who others wish for us to be? Here are five very common reasons.

Ignorance: Ignorance means to not know something. Think of the little boy who was raised in a family full of athletes. Since the moment he could walk, he was in football camp. He watched the game with his family on Sundays, played football with his friends on Saturdays, and was on a football team in school Monday through Friday. Whether anyone comes out and says anything to him about it, what do you believe he is going to perceive the expectation of him to be? What do you believe he is going to think others want/need him to be?

One may look at this word *ignorance* and think it to be negative, but, honestly, it is the best descriptor for why we may strive to meet others' needs. To answer concisely—we just do not know that we are doing it. We do not realize that it is happening. We may have been brainwashed since childhood, the brainwashing may have been very subtle while we were growing up, we may have gotten so used to it, we may have thought it to be honorable, and/or we may have been too busy striving to achieve … that we never had a free second to stop and question why we were on that path.

Love: Think about our partners. Whether it is expressed or unexpressed, they also have a desire for us to be a certain way. Think about the many times you have found yourself changing who you are or who you have always wanted to be for the sake of pleasing the man or the woman whom you love. Think of the many days when you had a choice on who you wanted to be today, and to appease the mood of your partner, you changed your plans and instead became who you felt he or she would most desire. We may strive to live up to what others want us to be and their expectations for us so that we can receive love from them. Love is a powerful thing, and that is why so many of us have an insatiable desire for it and are willing to do most things (including changing ourselves) to experience it.

Respect: Think about many leaders. One of the worst things that could happen to them would be to lose the respect of those who were at one time following their guidance in the workplace, in the community, and at home. In order to become a leader to the collective, you may be required to dress, talk, behave, and sound a certain way. How do you believe those in the workplace, community, and home need for one to dress, talk, sound, and behave in order to receive respect?

Many of us "change ourselves" because we have a desire to receive respect in return. Respect is a big one. It is admiration that is received because of who you are. People choose who to respect and disrespect based on what they perceive to be right and wrong. If they feel that you are right, you are respected. If they feel that what you are being, doing, or having is wrong, you may not be respected.

Acceptance: Do you remember the voracious desire you had to be accepted when you were growing up? How much of that has really gone away today? Perhaps it is still there but has gotten weaker. Perhaps this desire has gotten stronger. Naturally, we wish for others to receive us for who we are, but what happens if they don't? Most times, we may adjust a portion of who we are so that we are better received by others. Can you think of someone who does this? What about peer pressure you experience as a teenager? We may have a wish for others to receive us as a teen who chooses to be drug free, but in the desire to be a part of the in crowd, we may decide to try a substance at least once.

Being accepted is a real desire that should not be overlooked and should not be undervalued, because in it lies one of the biggest reasons we give away our power to others.

Material wealth: We see it all the time. We see those who have traded who they really desire to be in life in order to have material wealth: money and goods. Think about Robert Madoff. Do you think that he woke up one morning and said to himself, "Today, I choose to be hated by millions of Americans"? No, but he probably wanted to be rich and so he put aside morals and ethics in search of material gain. It happens more often than we would like to consider.

We hear the saying all the time. Money is *not* the root of all evil. The *love* of money is the root of all evil. I can clarify this saying even more. The *greed* for money is the root of all evil. Be careful that the decisions you are making regarding who you are choosing to be are authentic and are not based on greed of any sort.

Knowing who you are means accepting who you are choosing to be today, receiving it with appreciation, and courageously and authentically taking your choice everywhere you go.

Do not focus so much on the future, because the future will take care of itself. Being who you choose to be today (and doing this each day) can only make you the best and the happiest person you can be in your future.

It is very difficult to break free of who everyone else wishes you to be. Have you ever sat and wondered why you are on your current path? Is it because you really wanted it, or did someone else? Are you motivated to do what you are doing now because someone pushed you that way, or did you really feel inspired to do what you are currently doing? There are a lot of layers to this idea, and I do not expect you to pull them all back and uncover your true sense of self, want, and desire within the next three minutes. This will really require some soul searching. And if at the end of your journey, you discover that who everyone else wanted/needed you to be and who you desired to be were the same—*aligned*—then so be it. It makes your job moving forward only that much easier.

So, now that we have tackled who others want/need us to be, let us dive into our life situations, challenges, and obstacles. *Who do they want us to be?* I will explain in the next chapter.

End of Chapter Five
FOCUS
Family-Owned Chapter Understanding Segment

Current Experience

Teen: Pages [ ]: By now, your teen is learning about

Child: Pages [ ]: By now, your child has been introduced to

Conversational Topics

How do children, teens, and adults experience these feelings differently?

What prevents us from feeling aware of these things each moment of the day?

Exercises

As a family, ask your partner and children how many of these feelings—strong, powerful, creative, attractive, deserving, whole, loved—they have felt.

Which ones have they felt more strongly than others, and which are the weakest feelings for them? When do they feel these feelings most?

Discuss as a family how to grow in the awareness of each of these feelings as you progress through the day.

Actionable Items

As a family, come up with one simple affirmation that includes each of these things we are born with. Take a moment of appreciation each day during your reading of the affirmation.

My Journal

Chapter Six
The Struggle Part II: Who Your Situation Wants You to Be

> There is one constant in life — that is change, whether good or bad.
>
> —Phrantceena T. Halres

I heard Pastor T. D. Jakes on television once say that all it takes is to receive one phone call, one letter in the mail, one pink slip at work, and/or one knock at the door, and your entire life can change from that moment forward. We all go through things. That is no secret. I do not believe that one can ever truly be accustomed to going through situations. We try to rise above our financial challenges, our career challenges, our relationship challenges, our family challenges, and even our own internal challenges with self-esteem and fulfillment. We are trying to be resilient through each of these situations, and, believe me, it is not easy.

With each passing moment, there appears to be something that we are trying to work through. Some situations are tougher than others, and some people have more resources to work through those situations. Some of us get through certain situations faster than others for the same reasons. Going through tough times is one commonality that we all share, no matter our race, gender, financial status, creed, etc. We go through different situations at different levels and different intensities—*for different periods of time.*

Now, the conflict arises when you start to feel like your situation is actually your life. This often happens in two instances:

Extended situation: This occurs when you have been stuck in your situation for far too long and you are starting to feel like your situation is your life. You went from striving to overcome it, to wanting to overcome it, to feeling like you will never be able to overcome it, to accepting the situation as a part of your life—*and now a part of your identity.*

When does one go from being a person who happens to be without a home right now to being a homeless person? When does one go from being a person who happens to be low on funds to a poor person? Think of people who have lived in poverty for so long that they feel this is all their life was meant to be. Oftentimes, we do not take on an identity if we know that it will not be with us for too long.

Traumatic situation: This situation is not dependent on how long it lasts. It, instead, depends on the intensity of the matter and how much it consumes people during the intense period of time. These people did not have an opportunity to overcome it. It was almost as if it happened to them and they must deal with it. To these people, the situation becomes a matter of life and death.

Think of the man who is diagnosed with cancer. A situation like this can be so very intense that it can begin to consume every other aspect of your life. Situations that are so intense appear to leave very little time to think about anything else.

Regardless of whether a situation is extended or traumatic, have you ever wondered why we cannot seem to simply snap out of all of this?

> **Reminders:** How can we ever forget about anything when people around us continue to

remind us? Our situation continues to remind us. Everything we see is a deep reminder that we are still here, and we cannot seem to see beyond it.

Ignorance: We don't know that snapping out of the situation is an option, or we do not realize that we are snapped into it because we may be so busy day in and day out.

Desire: Believe it or not, some people prefer to stay in their situation because having anything change (for the better or worse) is scary.

Resources: Some do not have the resources readily available to them that are needed to come out of a situation. And to try to procure those resources takes a lot of time and effort that many do not want to invest. The unknown is scary. What if people stop helping me? What if people stop wanting me? What if people stop "seeing" me?

Situations have the ability to consume us like a black hole in space. If we are not fully aware of what is happening, situations can be given the power to infiltrate all other aspects of good in our life, leaving the appearance that we have nothing. It can make us feel as if we have nothing to give or receive. You can get locked in a trance in which you begin to believe that this is your life from now on. If this is you and you are in the middle of a situation, no matter how extended or intense it is, here are a few ways to successfully snap out of your own story.

Find light at end of the tunnel: "Don't wait for a light to appear at the end of the tunnel, stride down there and light the bloody thing yourself." I enjoy this quote by Sara Henderson. Take action to dig your way out of your situation if you have the ability. Think about the person with bad credit. It did not happen overnight. Nor can fixing it happen overnight. Sometimes it takes a little time, but a little action each day to repair what you perceive as broken is a good start.

Seek/ask for help: Open your mouth and let someone know that you need some help … whether it be assistance, therapy, prayer, or just good energy sent your way.

Find joy in what remains: "Birds sing after a storm; why shouldn't people feel as free to delight in whatever remains to them?" This is a quote from Rose Kennedy, and it makes a lot of sense. We can either focus on all that has been taken away from us, or focus on the blessings that remain. It is your choice.

Remember who you really are: In order to separate yourself from your situation, ask yourself, "Who am I in the midst of this situation?"

Answer: Who do you choose to be?

This is the most important remedy to prevent your situation from consuming you. Remembering who you really are means remembering to choose who you wish to be today, even in the midst of your turmoil, despair, and misery.

> **Knowing who you are means accepting who you are choosing to be today (regardless of your situation), receiving it with appreciation, and courageously and authentically taking your choice everywhere you go.**

Sometimes, a situation can be so consuming that you start to believe it is more powerful than it really is. You start to believe that who you are takes second priority to what you are going through. I tell people all the time that your situation wants you to believe that it is more than it is. It wants you to accept that it is more powerful than it really is.

Knowing who you are means knowing affirmatively that you are not your current situation. Your situation—*is your situation.* You are not an unemployed loser. You are "someone" (whoever you choose to be) who happens to be unemployed. You are not a burger flipper. You are "someone" (whoever you choose to be) who happens to flip burgers.

If your situation holds any power, it is only to teach you about who you can become. Who you are gets discovered when your back is against the wall and you are about to lose everything. It is the moment when all the chips are down, and you have to look your situation right in the eye and ask yourself who you wish to be in response to what is happening around or within you.

You are so much more than everything you experience. Are you starting to understand now? I certainly hope so, because now that you have a deep understanding of what it means to know who you are and to choose who you wish to be, we are about to embark on a fascinating journey of discovering exactly who you choose to be. Let's take action on creating our new, fascinating, and magnificent life—together!

The next part is about discovering yourself, creating more of yourself, and taking yourself on the road. Let's discover how!

End of Chapter Six
FOCUS
FAMILY-OWNED CHAPTER UNDERSTANDING SEGMENT

Current Experience
Teen: Pages [ ]: By now, your teen is learning about
Child: Pages [ ]: By now, your child has been introduced to

Conversational Topics
How do children, teens, and adults experience these feelings differently?

What prevents us from feeling aware of these things each moment of the day?

Exercises
As a family, ask your partner and children how many of these feelings—strong, powerful, creative, attractive, deserving, whole, loved—they have felt.

Which ones have they felt more strongly than others, and which are the weakest feelings for them? When do they feel these feelings most?

Discuss as a family how to grow in the awareness of each of these feelings as you progress through the day.

Actionable Items
As a family, come up with one simple affirmation that includes each of these things we are born with. Take a moment of appreciation each day during your reading of the affirmation.

My Journal

Part Two
Going to Somewhere

Chapter Seven
Do You Think You *Already* Know Who You Are?

It's time to awaken the giant within you.

—Phrantceena T. Halres

So maybe you've had an opportunity to read the first section and you believe that you already have a strong sense of who you are, or have a strong sense of self. You know that you do not fall into those categories, right? You know that no one can tell you who you are. I'd like to test that theory. I'd like to do a quiz with you. If you really already know who you are, I'd like for you to take some time to answer the following questions for me. Go ahead. I dare you!

Do you really know who you are?

1. If someone approached you and said that God does not love you because of your beliefs, you:

    a. Ignore them.

    b. Argue with them.

    c. Ask them what is necessary to believe in order for God to love you.

2. If you walked into a room where others were dressed the same, you would:

- a. Stop at the door, turn around, and run back home to change.
- b. Walk through the door shyly and awkwardly, trying to blend in as much as possible.
- c. Walk through the door carefree, comfortable in all that you've chosen to wear and compliment others on their great taste.

3. If you were told that you needed to change an aspect of your physical characteristics in order to get a contract, you:

   - a. Would really hear the person out. Maybe they have a point.
   - b. Make a list of who, what, and when the changes need to be made and get on it immediately.
   - c. Demonstrate the qualities that come from who you are that they may not have known about. Maybe you can make them love your differences!

So, there were only three questions. That was pretty simple. Right? These three questions and answers were fairly straightforward. I'm even sure that you probably recognized a pattern as you were taking the test. I'll bet you would now like to know how well you've scored. Ready?

Your score: There is no score to this quiz. The quiz was actually a test in and of itself.

Knowing who you are means that you do not have anything to prove to anyone. Feeling the need to take the quiz does not mean that you do not know who you are. If you did take the quiz, it was not meant to waste your time, but in fact, it was meant to show you how we all can get caught up very easily in trying to prove ourselves to someone else—even ourselves. The answers do not matter as much as the test alone. I want you to realize this. Knowing who you are means that you do not feel the need to explain yourself to anyone, let alone take a quiz to prove anything—*not even to me, the author*. People do this all the time. They throw in little quizzes or tests when you least expect it, and before you know it, you are headed down a path of explaining who you are. People can throw you off guard so quickly, and before you know it, you are explaining yourself to someone else. Try to not get caught up in such situations.

There is nothing you can be that would be right or wrong if it allowed you to experience both happiness and wholeness. Who you choose to be is your choice. Those who use the concept of knowing who you are most powerfully are those who do not feel a need to

> **Explain**: You do not feel the need to go back and forth to prove your position, to sway another's judgment, or to show others that they are wrong and you are right.
>
> **Stand in your own way.** Instead, you become your own cheerleader—rooting for your success.
>
> **Lose balance:** When you encounter turbulence, you know that you stand anchored in the truth.
>
> **Define yourself**: You no longer feel the need to be anyone or anything definitely. If you go from one venue to the next, you are fluid enough to change your sense of being as you desire.
>
> **Look externally**: You do not feel the need to look externally for all of your answers, because you

know that they reside within you. I am able to reflect the mirror back on me rather than constantly chasing someone or something else. Follow your heart instead of following seminars, sessions, and conferences where others are getting rich by delivering you information you already know within. You are not seeking saviors, and you instead become your own.

Get caught up: You no longer get caught up in one thing, but instead you catch the overall essence of what others are saying. For instance, you do not have to wear red in order to feel better, but you understand that wearing bright colors brings more positive energy your way.

Apologize: You are unapologetic about who you are. This is the most important aspect of knowing who you are. You can simply find peace in being, regardless of what happens to you externally.

If you find yourself being pulled into explaining yourself, return to chapter four and use those tools to move out of the situation. Pay attention, remember, understand, ignore, and educate. Knowing who you are takes being who you are. And being who you are takes discipline, desire, and dedication.

If you know who you are, then that is great. Help others to discover themselves. But for the rest of you who have not yet learned, the next chapter is especially for you. Together, let's discover who you are.

End of Chapter Seven

FOCUS
Family-Owned Chapter Understanding Segment

Current Experience

Teen: Pages [   ]: By now, your teen is learning about

Child: Pages [   ]: By now, your child has been introduced to

Conversational Topics

How do children, teens, and adults experience these feelings differently?

What prevents us from feeling aware of these things each moment of the day?

Exercises

As a family, ask your partner and children how many of these feelings—strong, powerful, creative, attractive, deserving, whole, loved—they have felt.

Which ones have they felt more strongly than others, and which are the weakest feelings for them? When do they feel these feelings most?

Discuss as a family how to grow in the awareness of each of these feelings as you progress through the day.

Actionable Items

As a family, come up with one simple affirmation that includes each of these things we are born with. Take a moment of appreciation each day during your reading of the affirmation.

My Journal

Chapter Eight
Discovering Who You Are

Focus on your strength, and know thy weakness.
—Phrantceena T. Halres

If you do not control your own destiny, others will! They will tell you what your potential is and push you to live up to it. Potential means having or showing the capacity to develop into something in the future. Your potential to *be* means having or showing the capacity to *be* whatever you desire. Did you know that most people listen to what others tell them to be because they have no clue as to what their highest potential is? Do you know your highest potential? We have mentioned this before, but what does it even mean for one to have a highest potential? If either were an easy question to answer, so many people would be living their highest potential right now.

What do you most desire? When I refer to your highest potential in this book, I am referring to your potential to be whatever you desire. Your potential to *be* is not just your potential to create your highest and best self each and every moment. Your potential to *be* is your potential to express your highest and best self—the side of you that has been there all along and is ready to be revealed. It is the light that has always been within you and is waiting to illuminate a room, a building, a city—*a world*!

You have the potential to

be excellent;

be authentic;

be powerful;

be talented;

be engaging;

be the best;

be exceptional;

be wonderful;

be gifted; and

be creative

And the list goes on and on. Your potential to *be* means being on the path you most desire, most connect to, and most flourish on. And knowing who you are is the start to being all that you were meant to be.

When people ask what steps they should take in order to discover who they are, I tell them a few things. First, I give them an exercise that I'd like to share with you. It is an exercise that will allow you to find quiet. This is the first step to discovering who you are.

- **Get quiet and breathe.**

    Let's discuss something that I call the conspiracy of quietness. In conspiracy of quietness, most will lead you to believe that you must find quiet. And in some cases (especially in the beginning)this is true. At a foundational level, we need to learn how to turn off all the distractions: television, cell phone, games, and other devices and activities. But at a higher level quiet comes from within, and regardless of where you are, it can be there. You can be in the midst of thebusiest airport in America and find quiet if you so choose. So take some time to find quiet. Breathe. Slow down your thoughts and actions. Breathe. With your eyes closed, ponder the answers to the questions below. Breathe.

When I feel that I am at my best, most joyful, and happiest,

- What am I doing?
- What am I thinking?
- How am I behaving?
- What am I wearing?
- What am I saying?
- Where am I, or where am I going?
- With whom (specifically) am I surrounding myself?
- What am I seeing?

- **Find awareness of the potential that is available to you.**
  - Qualities that were generational: Some people are raised knowing that their great-uncle Joe was an ethical man and that they are to be just like him. Those thoughts, examples, and environments have now grown embedded within you.

- Qualities you were born with: What were you born knowing just how to do? What is something that is known to be fairly difficult for others that comes pretty easily, naturally, and effortlessly to you? Are you an artist, a good speaker, or a natural counselor? Were you born knowing how to make others feel better, discovering easily the solutions to complex problems?

- Qualities others see in you: What characteristics do people most compliment you on?

- Qualities you see in yourself: Given your characteristics and abilities, what are you most thankful for?

- The answers to these questions will get you started on who you have the potential to be, but you also want to combine it with who you want to be.

- **Create and use affirmations.**
    - Speak as if things were already so. Use many "I am" affirmations.

- **Shift mentally through appreciation.**
    - All that you appreciate grows. Learn to see the beauty in everything around you. Once you see it, find appreciation in it.

- **Allow your spirit (intuition) to guide you.** Look for signs and confirmations of the guidance. It could be a book, for example, that grabs your attention and holds many of the answers to the questions you once had. It could be a conversation. When you are on a path, the world begins to teach and shape you. The world becomes your teacher.

- **Have nightly reflections.** What has worked for you today? What has not worked for you today? Use this information to make tomorrow an even better day for you.

- **Repeat the process each and every day.**

Try going against the gravity in your thinking. You now know a different you than you've known before. Learn to appreciate this newfound you that you've chosen to be. What you appreciate grows.

If you take all of these answers and combine them, then that is who you really are. All you need to do now is take action—be here. Be in a space where you are doing, thinking, behaving, wearing, saying, going, surrounding yourself with, and seeing what makes you feel at your best, most joyful, and happiest. Use your natural gifts and abilities, qualities that others see in you, and combine them with things that you see in yourself.

End of Chapter Eight

FOCUS
FAMILY-OWNED CHAPTER UNDERSTANDING SEGMENT

Current Experience
Teen: Pages [ ]: By now, your teen is learning about

Child: Pages [ ]: By now, your child has been introduced to

Conversational Topics
How do children, teens, and adults experience these feelings differently?

What prevents us from feeling aware of these things each moment of the day?

Exercises
As a family, ask your partner and children how many of these feelings—strong, powerful, creative, attractive, deserving, whole, loved—they have felt.

Which ones have they felt more strongly than others, and which are the weakest feelings for them? When do they feel these feelings most?

Discuss as a family how to grow in the awareness of each of these feelings as you progress through the day.

Actionable Items
As a family, come up with one simple affirmation that includes each of these things we are born with. Take a moment of appreciation each day during your reading of the affirmation.

My Journal

Chapter Nine
Fifteen Benefits in Knowing Who You Are

I am, that — I am, the way-truth and light.
—Phrantceena T. Halres

Why would anyone care to know who they are? Are there any significant benefits therein? As the title suggests, there is enormous power in knowing who you are. Let's discuss the top fifteen benefits.

1. **No one can tell you who you are.** No one will ever have the power again to tell you who you should be, how you should behave, or what you should believe.

2. **No one can tell you who you are not.** No one will ever have the power again to tell you who you will never be able to become.

3. **Life becomes simple.** "You mean that I do not have to buy her a dozen roses? All she really needs is for me to hold her hand in the park? Really?"

4. **You make better decisions.** You begin to make decisions that are better suited for what you desire. If your desire is to be happy, you will begin making decisions that promote happiness.

5. **The world opens up to you.** You attract people, places, and situations that are beneficial to you. Knowing who you are brings about positive energy. Positive energy attracts good things.

6. **You become aware of situations that are not beneficial to you.** You may still find yourself in situations that are not beneficial for you, but knowing who you are will allow you to feel more sensitively the negative energy and will increase your chances of walking away.

7. **You inspire others to discover who they really are.** No one wants to be unhappy and unsure in life all of the time. So when others see just how happy and full your life appears to be, they will want to know your secret. And some may even go as far as applying those secrets to their own life.

8. **You learn to appreciate and respect who others choose to be.** Now that you know the importance of and the power in making a choice, you find more appreciation and respect for those who have made their own choices in who they are. You grow to respect the sacredness in the process.

9. **You gain rhythm, balance, harmony, and alignment.** To be aligned feels good. It feels harmonious. You feel that the processes in your life are in sync. With this alignment you can start focusing on what you want to do now that you know who you are choosing to be.

10. **You can learn how to become more of you.** Knowing who you are brings more confidence, and this confidence brings more freedom to indulge in who you are choosing to be each day … and the cycle continues.

11. **There is a sense of peace in knowing who you are.** You no longer have to worry about who you were meant to be and whether the person you are is right or wrong. You gain a sense of freedom through the acceptance of knowing that you are in control of your own destiny.

12. **A positive aura develops.** You are able to create an aura of confidence, peace, and love when you know who you are. There is a soothing calm all around you once you give up chasing others' dreams, desires, and fears for you.

13. **You have courage to be more, do more ... have more.** You become impactful in life. When you know who you are, you discover that you have courage to do more with your life.

14. **You are not as easily swayed.** No one will be able to change your mind about who you are if you do not allow them to. Knowing who you are means accepting only those thoughts about you that align with who you choose to be.

15. **You become more resilient because your situation does not own you.** You start to find new ways of getting back up, dusting yourself off, and moving forward after a challenging experience, because you know that it is simply a bump in the road and not the road itself.

End of Chapter Nine

FOCUS
Family-Owned Chapter Understanding Segment

Current Experience

Teen: Pages [ ]: By now, your teen is learning about

Child: Pages [ ]: By now, your child has been introduced to

Conversational Topics

How do children, teens, and adults experience these feelings differently?

What prevents us from feeling aware of these things each moment of the day?

Exercises

As a family, ask your partner and children how many of these feelings—strong, powerful, creative, attractive, deserving, whole, loved—they have felt.

Which ones have they felt more strongly than others, and which are the weakest feelings for them? When do they feel these feelings most?

Discuss as a family how to grow in the awareness of each of these feelings as you progress through the day.

Actionable Items

As a family, come up with one simple affirmation that includes each of these things we are born with. Take a moment of appreciation each day during your reading of the affirmation.

My Journal

Chapter Ten
People Changers versus People Enhancers

> The only time we should look down on someone is when we are picking them up.
>
> —Phrantceena T. Halres

Up to this point, we've learned so many things about ourselves. We've learned who we are not, who others want us to be and why, and who we have the potential to be. But most importantly, we've begun learning how to discover who we are and the power that lies within that discovery.

In our self-discovery of who we are, we often run into others who wish to help us along the way. They want to give us advice on how to become who we wish to be. They've accepted us and now want to help us reach our goal. These are people who wish to bring good to our lives—and some successfully carry out this mission. But what makes one successful in their goodness and others not so successful? It all depends on whether someone is trying to change who you are (i.e., people changers) or simply enhance who you are (i.e., people enhancers). How can you tell the difference?

People changers are those who try to modify, adjust, or alter the person you have chosen to be in life. It almost feels rather daunting because they've made you believe beforehand that you were perfect. When someone attempts to change you, they are trying to tell you that who you are choosing to be is wrong, incorrect, or mistaken. It becomes very difficult to recognize them because they try to change you in what they call love, but often their advice is wrapped in their own fear, as we've discovered from earlier chapters. Here is how you can recognize people changers:

> **They create insecurity.** They make you question yourself and your decisions.
>
> **They confuse.** They make you wonder if you've made the right decision.
>
> **They remove.** They chip away at portions of you that you've chosen for yourself.
>
> **They impair.** They make you feel that you must depend on them in order to be better.
>
> **They change.** They make you feel as if you need to be different.

Always ask yourself, "How do I feel about myself when I leave this person?" Always trust your instincts.

People enhancers are those who assist in boosting, developing, and improving who you have chosen to be in life. They are the ones who appreciate who you are choosing to be, and they seek to know how they can assist you on your journey. They are the easiest ones to recognize because you are able to feel them and the positive impacts they have on your life. Here is how you can recognize people enhancers:

> **They increase.** They increase your energy, your level of inspiration, and your motivation to be yourself. They pour more love into your cup.

They cheer. They are very proud of you along the way.

They offer: Imagine a mentor who recommends that you join a speaking class. They do not want to change your choice to be a motivational speaker. They simply wish to enhance your speaking ability. They do not wish to take away from who you are. They instead bring offerings in the forms of material substances, ideas, and emotional support that enhance who you wish to be.

They inspire. They leave you feeling like you can be, do, and have much more in life.

They clarify. It is a fact that wearing the right pair of glasses can drastically improve one's vision. Glasses create a clear display that does not change what you see, but how you see it. People enhancers clarify one's vision of who they choose to be. They remove the glasses, clean them, and place them back on you, having removed all specks and spots that were once there.

Always ask yourself, "How do I feel about myself when I leave this person?" Always trust your instincts.

You do not have to run from people changers. Ironically, you'll find that many of them are those who love us most but just do not realize that they are trying to change who we are. And we often go wrong with people changers by trying to change their minds, prove them wrong, and/or argue with them.

I recommend that you avoid trying to change a people changer's mind by trying to prove them wrong. At the end of the day, it becomes a waste of energy that could be best spent in knowing more about who you are and who you choose to be.

So, what options do we have in dealing with people changers?

Outer circle. Just because they are friends or loved ones does not mean that they deserve all of your time and space. You can check in on them as you deem appropriate.

Listen and show respect. Most people just want to be heard. When you are talking to people changers, simply listen to what they are saying, show respect for their opinion, and allow the discussion to fizzle out on its own. You do not have to verbally disagree. Simply saying, "I understand what you are saying," will often suffice.

So now that we've figured out how to maneuver around people changers, let's spend some time discussing people whom I enjoy giving most of my time to—people enhancers.

What if you do not know any people enhancers? Where can you go to find them? You can find them hanging around other people enhancers. Ask for recommendations. Get a referral. Also, take some time and go to inspirational and or motivational networking functions. And once you find them, here are two things that you can do immediately that could forever change your life.

Surround yourself by them. E-mail them. Call them. Invite them to lunch, and soak up the wisdom they have to offer.

Become one. Give back. Whatever you give out to the world, you will also receive.

End of Chapter Ten
FOCUS
Family-Owned Chapter Understanding Segment

Current Experience

Teen: Pages [ ]: By now, your teen is learning about

Child: Pages [ ]: By now, your child has been introduced to

Conversational Topics

How do children, teens, and adults experience these feelings differently?

What prevents us from feeling aware of these things each moment of the day?

Exercises

As a family, ask your partner and children how many of these feelings—strong, powerful, creative, attractive, deserving, whole, loved—they have felt.

Which ones have they felt more strongly than others, and which are the weakest feelings for them? When do they feel these feelings most?

Discuss as a family how to grow in the awareness of each of these feelings as you progress through the day.

Actionable Items

As a family, come up with one simple affirmation that includes each of these things we are born with. Take a moment of appreciation each day during your reading of the affirmation.

My Journal

Chapter Eleven
Being Yourself Fully versus Becoming More of Who You Are

Be all of you.

—Phrantceena T. Halres

My name means "Freedom & Liberation" andused to be spelled Francina Y.Tate-Harris, with Tate as my maiden name, Harris being my ex-husband's last name. As I began talking with a dear friend, I was educated on the energy that a name sends. I would often wonder, "What's in a name?" How powerful are names in the grand scheme of our lives? She taught me to better understand that a remarkable level of energy comes with the name one is given. With that, I decided to change the "spelling" of my name from Francina Tate Harris to Phrantceena T. Halres. There is energy in a name, and I was pleased with this change. Knowing what I am is one level; expressing who I am is another. This name change was a significant way that I used to express & protect myself.

There are differences among being who you are, living who you are fully, and becoming more of yourself. You may have thought that knowing who you are is all there is, but so many amazing opportunities await you when you are able to learn how to live who you are and also express who you are. The best way to understand the differences is to discuss them in terms of levels. Level one is knowing who you are, or *creating yourself*. Level two is living who you are, or *experiencing yourself*. Level three is becoming more of who you are, or *expressing yourself*.

Level one: Creating yourself

Level two: Living yourself

Level three: Expressing yourself

Creating yourself: Knowing who you are is to proclaim, "This is who I choose to be—*everywhere I go!*"

Knowing yourself is to be what is real and authentic to you. It is the same thing as embracing who you are. It means that your behavior, desires, and thoughts are aligned with the person you are choosing to be in the moment.

My pledge: I choose to be Phrantceena Halres. I choose to be free, at peace, in harmony, and full of love everywhere I go.

Living yourself: Living who you are is to ask, "What can I do to experience myself?"

People experience themselves in everything they do. The difference is that you can now experience the person you are choosing to be instead of the person others have pushed you into being. In order to experience who you are, you can do things like take classes, redecorate, network, and befriend those who are very similar to who you are choosing to be.

My pledge: I choose experience myself by meditating, traveling, and allowing myself to be further educated in areas that bring joy to me.

Expressing yourself: Becoming more of who you are is to proclaim, "Now that I am finally myself and loving it, *what can I do with it?*"

Becoming more of who you are is to do something with the person you've chosen to be. You now wish to give yourself to the world in some way. Some do this as philanthropists, some as business owners, and others as artists who can give themselves back to the world through singing, dancing, acting, or painting/drawing. Some simply pray for the world to be a better place. Thank God for all of them!

My pledge: I choose to express myself through writing, speaking, and traveling the globe in order to help others break free from the social ties that bind. Thereby, I am helping others to have a fuller, more whole style of living.

Now that you've learned that there are deeper levels to experiencing yourself, I would advise following the steps in order. It would be detrimental, for example, to try to become more, or to try to experience yourself, if you are not first certain of who or what you'd like to be. Also, try to engage others in assisting you at each level. The more, the merrier. People can give you great ideas and suggestions in how to further experience yourself, and they will be there to support you if you wish to help others.

There is something else that I'd like to leave with you before closing this chapter. Always know that although changing one's name is a profound, life-changing, and symbolic experience, you do not have to change your name in order to further experience yourself. It is enough to simply know who you are choosing to be in life and to be that person. Nothing more needs to be done—unless you'd like to do more. There is no competition—no one to compete against. There is only you, in harmony, in joy, and in peace.

End of Chapter Eleven
FOCUS
FAMILY-OWNED CHAPTER UNDERSTANDING SEGMENT

Current Experience
Teen: Pages [ ]: By now, your teen is learning about

Child: Pages [ ]: By now, your child has been introduced to

Conversational Topics
How do children, teens, and adults experience these feelings differently?

What prevents us from feeling aware of these things each moment of the day?

Exercises
As a family, ask your partner and children how many of these feelings—strong, powerful, creative, attractive, deserving, whole, loved—they have felt.

Which ones have they felt more strongly than others, and which are the weakest feelings for them? When do they feel these feelings most?

Discuss as a family how to grow in the awareness of each of these feelings as you progress through the day.

Actionable Items
As a family, come up with one simple affirmation that includes each of these things we are born with. Take a moment of appreciation each day during your reading of the affirmation.

My Journal

Chapter Twelve
Taking Who You Are on the Road

No matter where you go, there you are.

—Unknown

Here is an interesting dilemma that is experienced very often. Most people believe that by a simple change of their location, their partners, or even their career, they will be happier in life. But this is true only if it truly is your location, your partner, or your career that made you unhappy in the first place. Most people would change these things and within six months would find themselves in a deep state of unhappiness all over again. Why does this so frequently happen?

I will state the answer very simply. Everywhere you go, *there you are*.

Our world is filled with going places. Some trips are less eventful than others because often we may go on them alone. For instance, we go to the gym, we go to the grocery store, we go to visit the dentist, and we go to bed at night. We do these things so consistently and frequently that it is simple for us to take this show on the road. Since we are going at these things alone no one is really trying to force us to do anything differently.

But what about those moments when we are going to work, going to socialize or network, going on a date, or even going to a family gathering? Those experiences are very eventful, aren't they? They are very eventful and exhausting. It is not simply the event that is taking place, but it is the energy that it takes to become who others expect you to be that requires the most energy and goodness—it is tiring!

But do not despair. You can make this situation work for you. If you have been successful enough to create the person you've always wanted to be, then this same adage works in the exact same manner. The person that you are today can go with you everywhere you want to be. That is right! You can take this show on the road, and I'd like to take an opportunity to show you how. Are you ready?

Let's start here. If everywhere you go, there you are, then *make sure to be happy with that person*. Make sure you are happy with *you*. When you truly know who you are, you will always work toward choosing the path that best serves the person you wish to be, everywhere you are.

Many people ask me the following questions:

- How do I find love without sacrificing who I am choosing to be?
- How do I get a job offer without sacrificing who I am choosing to be?
- How do I get friends without sacrificing who I am choosing to be?
- How do I become a great leader without sacrificing who I am choosing to be?
- How do I build an audience/platform without sacrificing who I am choosing to be?

These are all such great questions! I'm so glad they are being asked. If you are happy with who you are, do not change. That is rule number one. Always know who you are when you make a decision. That is rule number two. Many people allow a situation to become larger than who they are. In other words, they begin to lose sight of themselves under certain conditions. In these instances, they give themselves (*their power*) away for something that they feel is greater (*the situation*). Many people give up who they are for a relationship, for a promotion, for friends, and for audiences. It's been happening so long that it almost feels natural. Many stand on the sidelines with one hand outstretched releasing who they are and reaching for something they feel is more valuable.

Always remember that nothing is more valuable than living joyfully. If who you are choosing to be leaves you feeling your highest, happiest, most joyful, and connected, and someone (or a group of people) does not accept you because of this, then simply allow them to go. What is the point in having the relationship, the job, the friends, and the audience if you are unhappy with who you are? With that, allow the date, the promotion, the job offer, the friends, and the platform to go. Release them with love because everywhere you go, there you are. Believe me. I know that you must be saying, "Easier said than done!" but if you must change what makes you most happy (who you are), then is whatever you are reaching out for worth it? There will be other lovers, job offers, promotions, friends, and audiences who will love and accept who you are, just as you are.

There is one exception to this rule, however. When you take who you are on the road, do so fully, but be sure that who you are choosing to be does not prevent others from being who they are choosing to be. Try not to allow who you are to affect other people negatively. Be sensitive to the energy that you are putting out into the world. Everyone can feel your energy, whether or not you realize it—even those who cannot tell you, because they cannot speak. Do not let your choice in who you are pigeonhole another person. Do not allow it to hold back other people. Use your power for good. Let who you are inspire others. Let it motivate others.

At the end of the day, it is not difficult to take you everywhere you go! It requires more energy to hide or mask your true nature. So do not hide your pretty smile, your quirks, your intelligence, and your eccentricities. Show them off authentically! Show them off unapologetically.

But now, what do you do when who you are changes—*again*?

End of Chapter Twelve
FOCUS
Family-Owned Chapter Understanding Segment

Current Experience
Teen: Pages [ ]: By now, your teen is learning about

Child: Pages [ ]: By now, your child has been introduced to

Conversational Topics
How do children, teens, and adults experience these feelings differently?

What prevents us from feeling aware of these things each moment of the day?

Exercises
As a family, ask your partner and children how many of these feelings—strong, powerful, creative, attractive, deserving, whole, loved—they have felt.

Which ones have they felt more strongly than others, and which are the weakest feelings for them? When do they feel these feelings most?

Discuss as a family how to grow in the awareness of each of these feelings as you progress through the day.

Actionable Items
As a family, come up with one simple affirmation that includes each of these things we are born with. Take a moment of appreciation each day during your reading of the affirmation.

My Journal

Part Three
Now Here, Now What?

Chapter Twelve
When Who You Are Changes, Again

Evolution is a necessary part of you.
—Phrantceena T. Halres

You've already changed once, right? At one time you were a slow-moving caterpillar whose only focus was getting from one place to the next. You didn't know who you were. You didn't even know that creating what you wanted to be was an option. But now look at you. You've evolved into a beautiful butterfly that can't be held down, because you choose to be free, at peace, and in harmony with all of life. You've set a path for yourself, and you feel very good and confident about it. You know who you wish to be, and you are moving full speed ahead to all that you desire. And that is a wonderful state of being.

But a year later, something happens. All that you thought you wanted is not as interesting to you. All that you thought you would be is now wanting to be different. You have an overwhelming fear that you are changing—again.

And in reality you are. You are evolving.

Again, you return to being the caterpillar who has fears of the unknown. You resist the thought of changing again, because you fear that you may

End up looking different. You may sound different, dress differently, walk differently … behave differently. You fear that you may become foreign to who you've always been.

Have to fly away. You fear that you may have to leave what has been most comfortable and safe to you.

Desire new things. You fear that you may not want what you wanted in your past. It could be as small as the desire to discontinue drinking coffee, or it could be as large is your desire to find a new partner with whom to share your life.

I wish for all of you to know that knowing who you are is not a static concept. It is an evolution. It is not a one-time learning experience you go through and then you are done. Just as your taste buds change and your decisions change, so too will your definition of who you are change. And do you want to know something else?

It is okay …
Evolution is part of the process of life. It is a part of living. You need only to trust this process. Understanding how to "trust the process" is a concept that will be further explained in an upcoming chapter, but for now all you need to understand is that you are being supported. You are loved. You are being taken care of. Simply trust that there is a greater plan for your life.

Please know that it is okay to change as long as you are doing it for the right reasons. Refer to chapter four for a deeper description of the wrong reasons to change. The change process is not an easy one. Just as it was in the beginning for you, this evolution can be confusing and frustrating, and it can cause a little anxiety because, after all, who likes change? You were once very happy and content, knowing exactly who you wanted to be, and now you must feel as if you are at square one again. I'm sorry that you are experiencing this situation, but simply remember that if you were a beautiful butterfly at your last metamorphosis, imagine your beauty during this next one.

Here are some helpful steps to better assist you through your process of evolution:

Step one: *Expect the change.*

Change is inevitable. Evolution is not. Your taste buds can signal to you that you want something different, but it is up to you to act on it. The desire to grow is inevitable; the actual growth is up to you.

Step two: *Allow the change.*

Let change happen. There is a reason you feel the way you do now. You feel unsettled or unhappy because something within you is desiring expression. If it will make you feel more peaceful and happy, it must be released.

Step three: *Understand the change.*

Why do you feel this way? Did something happen? Did something not happen? There is a lesson behind what you are now desiring or not desiring. Try to understand it so that you are able to grow from it.

Step four: *Embrace the change.*

Accept the change. Do not resist it. Do not fight it. How can you fight reality? That is as crazy as trying to fight the air. Whether you like it or not, it is there. If you are unable to embrace it now, it is okay. Simply work on perfecting steps one through three until you feel more comfortable working through this step.

Step five. *Appreciate the change.*

Seek reasons to love what is happening. Even if the only reason is that you are happy, appreciate the change because it was able to bring happiness your way that was not there before.

And when the change is completed, try to surround yourself with others who respect your change, just as you did the first time you began learning who you are. No one has to expect, allow, understand, embrace, or appreciate the change. That is your job. If others take the initiative to do these things, that is a bonus. All others must only respect it in order to remain in your circle of trust.

Evolution can be a beautiful thing when we allow ourselves the freedom, the time, and the space to evolve.

End of Chapter Thirteen
FOCUS
Family-Owned Chapter Understanding Segment

Current Experience

Teen: Pages [ ]: By now, your teen is learning about

Child: Pages [ ]: By now, your child has been introduced to

Conversational Topics

How do children, teens, and adults experience these feelings differently?

What prevents us from feeling aware of these things each moment of the day?

Exercises

As a family, ask your partner and children how many of these feelings—strong, powerful, creative, attractive, deserving, whole, loved—they have felt.

Which ones have they felt more strongly than others, and which are the weakest feelings for them? When do they feel these feelings most?

Discuss as a family how to grow in the awareness of each of these feelings as you progress through the day.

Actionable Items

As a family, come up with one simple affirmation that includes each of these things we are born with. Take a moment of appreciation each day during your reading of the affirmation.

My Journal

Chapter Fourteen
When You Forget Who You Are

> You never lose who you are. You either forget, or you fail to choose.
>
> —Phrantceena T. Halres

The truth is that there will be times when you forget how beautiful, how wonderful, how whole and complete you truly are. As a matter of fact, there will be moments when you will forget all of chapter 1 … *if you haven't already.* You won't remember that you once believed you (*as was taught in chapter 1*) were born to be strong, powerful, creative, attractive, deserving, beautiful, and loved. Times will come when you will have amnesia and once again feel the struggles of an unhappy and incomplete life.

What will you do then? What do you do when you completely forget who you are?

But before we answer this question, I'd like to ask another very important question. What causes us to forget who we are? The answer is, you forget who you are when your life becomes imbalanced—*shifted against your will.* For some, it may seem their life has been turned upside down; for others, it may be that their life is just on shaky ground right now. For example:

Future unknown: You may have just gotten a diagnosis that was unexpected. You may have learned that your company is downsizing. You may have even gotten word that your child was suddenly rushed to the hospital. *What does this mean for the future?*

Hypnosis: Some people are such great manipulators that they can completely talk you out of believing who you are. You may have been the victim of verbal abuse or neglect.

Failure: When we perceive or feel failure, we have been conditioned to acquiest to it.

Disconnection: Ending a connection with someone you once loved, like a spouse or a friend, can create a shift in your life that was unexpected.

Tragedy: What if another hurricane like Hurricane Katrina hits your hometown tomorrow? What if another 9/11 happens tomorrow? What if it is your child's description on the next Amber Alert? Such events can bring an absolute shift in what was once a very balanced and peaceful life.

Overall, life can hit you fast. And if you are not prepared, situations like these can easily throw you off balance. Such situations can create confusion that makes you question many things, including yourself. It is great if you can remember who you are when things are working well in your life, but the most remarkable people to me are the ones who remember who they are when all hope seems to be gone, when their back is up against the wall—*when all they have left is faith.* They are truly my heroes.

Now that we know what common situations can cause us to forget who we are, let's return to the initial question.

What do you do when you forget who you are?

Answer: You create yourself all over again ... in the midst of your tragedy, disconnection, or unknown future. Ask yourself, "Who do I want to be in the midst of this?"

Your answer to this question help you remember that you can create who you wish to be at every moment of the day. As a matter of fact, this is what I consider "failing forward." Use what has just happened in your life to propel you in a new direction. Instead of falling backward, use what you are learning about the situation and about yourself to move forward. I am a firm believer that things do not happen *to* us. They happen *for* us. And if you totally let go of who you are when you experience an unknown future, a disconnection, a failure, or a tragedy, then you are missing the whole point of its occurrence. Situations cause ripples in our lives in order to help us to further evolve. These ripples thrust us into a new state of awareness. We become aware that life is too short, of what matters most, and of who and what are most important.. These ripples in our lives allow us to better feed our soul. If your soul wishes to grow, where is this situation telling you to focus your attention? Think of it this way. If my soul is hungry, what outcome from this situation would most feed it?

Here are some other neat questions to ask yourself:

- What can this situation teach me about myself and others?
- What sunshine can I add to what seems to be darkness right now?
- How was I prepared for this situation, and how can I be better prepared if it happens again?

Have you even considered keeping a proof journal? You write in this journal only when you are at your highest and feeling the best about yourself. When you are in this space, seek proof of who you really are and write about it in your journal. If you'd like to take it one step further, cut out photos, and add quotes and affirmations that are most meaningful to you. This way, when you forget who you are, you can go back to this journal not only for a reminder, but also for proof that you were once that person; it will give you inspiration and motivation to once again be him or her.

Even in the midst of what may appear to be one of life's most challenging situations, do not forget who you are. And if you do, simply create who you wish to be as a result of this situation. Your foundation is built on either sand or concrete, and life will very quickly teach you which one it is.

End of Chapter Fourteen
FOCUS
Family-Owned Chapter Understanding Segment

Current Experience

Teen: Pages [ ]: By now, your teen is learning about

Child: Pages [ ]: By now, your child has been introduced to

Conversational Topics

How do children, teens, and adults experience these feelings differently?

What prevents us from feeling aware of these things each moment of the day?

Exercises

As a family, ask your partner and children how many of these feelings—strong, powerful, creative, attractive, deserving, whole, loved—they have felt.

Which ones have they felt more strongly than others, and which are the weakest feelings for them? When do they feel these feelings most?

Discuss as a family how to grow in the awareness of each of these feelings as you progress through the day.

Actionable Items

As a family, come up with one simple affirmation that includes each of these things we are born with. Take a moment of appreciation each day during your reading of the affirmation.

My Journal

Chapter Fifteen
Helping Others Discover Who They Are

> You can lead a horse to water, but you cannot make it drink.
>
> —Unknown

To help people discover who they are is to help them discover their potential. But as this is such a delicate area of discussion, I'd like to tread very lightly. You'll understand what I mean in a moment.

We've all done it. We've seen potential in other people, and we've tried our best to help them to reach that potential. I can think of several times that I tried to do this with my youngest sister. She has always been the closest to me of all my siblings. Because of that, I used to try to push her to rise to the potential that I felt she had. It took a long time for me to realize that her reaching her potential is none of my business. My goal is not to force her to be what I think she should be. My only responsibility is to reach *my* potential, and if she is inspired along the way, *that's a bonus.*

I am sharing this story with you because I think that many people can relate to it. For those whom we love, it is very hard to sit back and watch them not live what we would consider to be a happy and full life. It is heartbreaking to achieve so much in your life and to watch others struggle. It almost gets to the point where you want to do "it" for them. It can be whatever they are not doing that you think would help them know who they are, live it, and then express it.

In attempting to help others discover who they are, it is very important that you remember three things. First, a person's potential isn't really any of your business. As harsh as it may sound, this idea will help ease a lot of the stress you are feeling (*in trying to push the person to reach it*) and the stress that you are placing on the other person (*in trying to push him or her to reach it*). It is great that you see potential in others and that you share what you see with them, but who they become is up to them. It is completely their business. Second, some people have more issues in their lives than others do. They may not be ready for your assistance or support at this time. You must meet people where they are and not where you think they are or wish they were. The third thing is what I call my airplane safety message. Save yourself first before saving others. Focus on being the change you wish to see in the world and walking the talk fully before you try to save the rest of the world.

With that being said, here are six things you should never do in attempting to help other people discover who they are.

1. **Judge them.** Do not give your opinion on who they are choosing to be if it hinders their growth. Inspire them.

2. **Force them.** Do not force someone to become who you wish for them to be. Inspire them.

3. **Change them.** Do not try to change someone into who you wish for them to be. Inspire them.

4. **Criticize them.** Do not criticize someone's efforts toward being who they choose to be. Inspire them.

5. **Enable them.** Do not enable people who are not choosing to live up to their own potential. Inspire them.

6. **Give up on them.** Do not turn your back on people simply because they have not yet discovered their potential. Continue to inspire them.

> Give a man a fish, feed him for a day. Teach a man to fish, feed him for a lifetime.
>
> —Unknown

I love this part. Here is where we answer the million-dollar question. How can I help others to discover who they are?

Inspire them. I know you've seen this one coming from a mile away. Lead by example. Be the change you wish to see. Show them that it is possible to live a happy and fulfilling life. Encourage positive change. You know the motto, "When you see something, say something!" If you see that they are doing something for themselves that is making them happier in life, encourage them to keep up the good work. Be a dedicated and loud cheerleader in their lives. Everyone needs encouragement to keep up the good fight. Cheer them on. And most of all, be authentic in all of your efforts to inspire others to discover who they really are. Even a three-year-old can sense whether someone is being fake or authentic.

"Live it, be it, bring it" is my motto. People are attracted to it. People will be attracted to your light the way moths are attracted to a flame. Remind people that they do not need to go anywhere to get to a light. There is nothing to chase. We are already there. It is already within us.

End of Chapter Fifteen
FOCUS
Family-Owned Chapter Understanding Segment

Current Experience

Teen: Pages [ ]: By now, your teen is learning about

Child: Pages [ ]: By now, your child has been introduced to

Conversational Topics

How do children, teens, and adults experience these feelings differently?

What prevents us from feeling aware of these things each moment of the day?

Exercises

As a family, ask your partner and children how many of these feelings—strong, powerful, creative, attractive, deserving, whole, loved—they have felt.

Which ones have they felt more strongly than others, and which are the weakest feelings for them? When do they feel these feelings most?

Discuss as a family how to grow in the awareness of each of these feelings as you progress through the day.

Actionable Items

As a family, come up with one simple affirmation that includes each of these things we are born with. Take a moment of appreciation each day during your reading of the affirmation.

My Journal

Chapter Sixteen
Trusting Yourself, Trusting Others

> Trust yourself first.
>
> —Phrantceena T. Halres

The most significant part of knowing who you are is understanding how to trust. Trust is one of the hardest things to do because it requires having faith in something that is unseen. This trust is ultimately the faith that things are happening for your good and for your growth. Think of all that you've read so far. You must have faith not only that you were you born to be creative, loved, attractive, deserving, beautiful, whole, powerful, and strong, but also that you have the ability to produce all of those things in the present tense. You must carry the faith that you can remember who you are when things are going great and also when calamity strikes. You must have faith to be able to walk down the street being who you are choosing to be and know that it is okay. Do you remember what it means to know who you are?

Knowing who you are means accepting who you are choosing to be today, receiving it with appreciation, and taking your choice authentically and boldly everywhere you go.

This takes trust. Trust takes an enormous amount of faith. In knowing who you are you must learn to trust yourself, trust others, and trust the process. None of the three is a simple endeavor.

Trusting yourself. You must trust that what makes you happy—*what makes you genuinely and sincerely happy in life*—will not lead you in the wrong direction. You must trust that it will lead you in a very perfect and divine direction. When did we get to the point where we were afraid to follow what makes us happy in life? At the end of the day, your happiness is the only compass that you need. The expression "follow your heart" has become so watered down that many do not understand what it means. But what if I were to say, "Follow what makes you happy"? Although some would have to ponder this idea a little longer than others, depending on how out of touch you've been with yourself lately, I'm sure most would tell you the direction they need to go.

When was the last time you truly trusted yourself?

Trusting others. This is the type of trust in the world. Your trust is that the world will rise up to meet you where you are and that all other people, places, and things that do not support who you are will fall away. When you trust others, you are trusting that they will be who they say they are and that if you let them into your circle of love, they will be good stewards of this trust. Trusting others also starts with trusting yourself. In order to trust others, people must first believe that they are good judges of character. Believe that you are, and you will learn to become a good judge of character.

When was the last time you truly trusted others?

Trusting the process. Do you remember we talked about *trusting the process* in chapter thirteen? When I refer to the process, I am referring to the life process. I hope you grasp the notion that everything that is happening around you is happening *for* you and not *to* you. When something happens to you, you become a victim. When something happens for you, you become a chosen one. Wouldn't you prefer to be a chosen one? Things happen in life that assist evolution; otherwise, many of us would be in the same place today that we were in twenty years ago. Think about your first love, whether you were in grade school or in college, or whether it was last year. What if your heart was never broken? Where would you be today?

When was the last time you truly trusted the process of life?

Have you noticed that trusting becomes increasingly difficult as you move down the list? You go from trusting yourself (as if this isn't hard enough) to trusting others, to finally trusting "the process." Do you know why this is? You are moving further outside of your span of control. For the most part, you cannot control others, and you most certainly cannot control the process of life. When it comes to you, you can think back to past experiences when you may have made decisions that were not for the best and the highest for you; so now you must learn how to trust that you will not do that in the future. When it comes to others, you do not know their true intentions or motives, and this can be pretty frightening. And as for trusting the process, you cannot see into the future, so you have no clue as to what it holds.

As I began to wrap up this chapter, I found myself asking the question, "Why does anyone need to trust themselves, trust others, and trust the process in order to have a successful life?" Why are these things so important to knowing who you are? Now, I know that if this question occurred to me, the author, it must also be on your mind as the reader. And the answer came to me suddenly ...

It takes a lot of energy to not trust. It takes a lot of time to not trust. This time could be much better spent enjoying your life. For every time you don't trust yourself, another, or the process of life, much of your time goes to worrying, fretting, removing, and disconnecting. Negative energy pours into your life the more you distrust. But when you learn to trust, positive energy prevails and you spend your time creating, loving, adding, and connecting.

Trust is a beautiful thing if you allow it to be.

End of Chapter Seventeen

FOCUS
Family-Owned Chapter Understanding Segment

Current Experience
Teen: Pages [ ]: By now, your teen is learning about

Child: Pages [ ]: By now, your child has been introduced to

Conversational Topics
How do children, teens, and adults experience these feelings differently?

What prevents us from feeling aware of these things each moment of the day?

Exercises
As a family, ask your partner and children how many of these feelings—strong, powerful, creative, attractive, deserving, whole, loved—they have felt.

Which ones have they felt more strongly than others, and which are the weakest feelings for them? When do they feel these feelings most?

Discuss as a family how to grow in the awareness of each of these feelings as you progress through the day.

Actionable Items
As a family, come up with one simple affirmation that includes each of these things we are born with. Take a moment of appreciation each day during your reading of the affirmation.

My Journal

Chapter Seventeen
Conclusion

The love you seek is within you.
—Phrantceena T. Halres

Dear friends, I am forever grateful for the time that you've spent with me on this portion of our journey. The things I've shared with you are from the heart, and it is all a part of my vision in giving you back to yourself. It is my sincere desire that you feel the love that has poured over each of these pages. My goal is to shift Maslow's hierarchy of needs in order to demonstrate how seeking self-actualization first can transform everything else. In other words, when you know who you are, everything else falls in line. When you know who you are, you have higher self-esteem. When you have higher self-esteem, people tend to become more attracted to you and to want to be connected to you. The more people that you have who love and support you, the safer you begin to feel in life … and the safer you feel in life, the more you'll feel supported in having your physiological needs met.

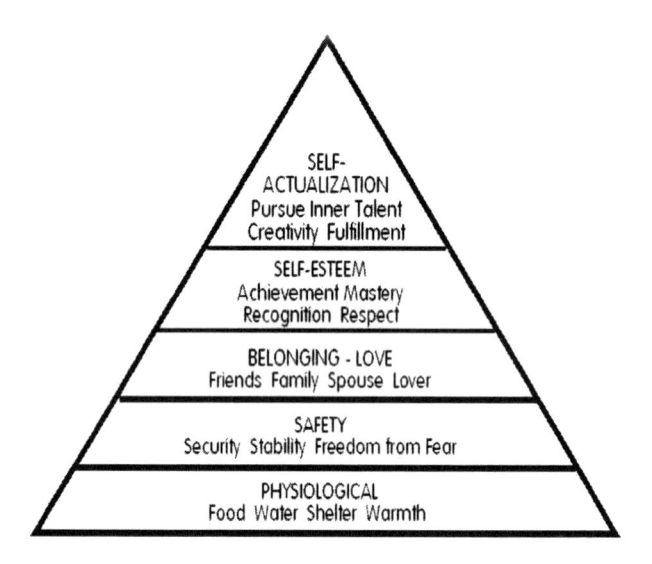

```
                    SELF-
                 ACTUALIZATION
               Pursue Inner Talent
              Creativity Fulfillment
              SELF-ESTEEM
           Achievement Mastery
           Recognition Respect
          BELONGING - LOVE
       Friends Family Spouse Lover
               SAFETY
     Security Stability Freedom from Fear
            PHYSIOLOGICAL
         Food Water Shelter Warmth
```

As a matter of fact, the entire system changes when people know who they are. Think of mothers, fathers, daughters, sons, teachers, religious figureheads, and politicians. If everyone understood the importance of knowing who they are, people would be much happier. We could perhaps move to a free enterprise of self-categorization. No one would feel the need to place labels on others, and they would allow others to best define themselves.

So, now that you have a better understanding of who you are and the power to create exactly what you wish to be in life, I'd like to connect you to the next book in this series.

Strength: The Art of Holding Your Internal Power through External Crises
Welcome to my second creed within the *I Am* series. I am strength. With this next book, allow me to walk you through what it means to have internal power and how to use it when crises seem to prevail all around you. In book number two, there is so much to talk

about. We have so much more work to do, but the blessing is that we can do it together.

Until we meet again, my wish for you will always remain the same. Giving you back to yourself is the best gift that one can give, and I hope that this book and those that follow help remind you of how magnificent you really are and how amazing you can be every day of your life.

A Wonderful Reminder ...

While praying one day, a little girl asked,

"Who are you, Lord?"

He answered, "I Am"

But Who is I Am?" she said.

And He replied …"I Am Love, I Am Peace,

I Am Grace, I Am Joy,

I Am the Way, Truth and the Light,

I Am the Comforter,

I Am Strength, I Am Power

I Am Shelter, I Am ProtectionI Am the Creator;

I Am the Beginning and the End,

I Am the Most High."

The girl with tears in her eyes looked

Toward heaven and said,

"Now I understand, but Lord, Who Am I?"

Then God tenderly wiped the tears

From her eyes and whispered,

"You are mine."

—Phrantceena T. Halres